CHILDREN IN HISTORY
The Egyptians

Fiona Macdonald

FRANKLIN WATTS
LONDON•SYDNEY

First published in 2009 by
Franklin Watts
338 Euston Road
London NW1 3BH

Franklin Watts Australia
Level 17/207 Kent Street
Sydney, NSW 2000

ISBN 978 0 7496 8702 1
Dewey classification: 693

Series Editor: Jeremy Smith
Art director: Jonathan Hair
Design: Jane Hawkins
Picture research: Diana Morris

A CIP catalogue record for this book is available
from the British Library

Franklin Watts is a division of Hachette Children's
Books, an Hachette
UK company.
www.hachette.co.uk

Printed in China

Contents

Introduction

Egypt was home to the most famous and long-lasting civilization in the ancient world. Egyptian kings - known as 'pharaohs' - first linked several small states into one strong kingdom around 3100 BCE.

Kingdom on the Nile

Egypt's wealth came from the mighty River Nile. The longest river in the world, it flooded the land on either side of its banks every year, bringing life-giving water and rich, fertile mud. In riverside fields, Egyptian farmers grew grain to feed their families and pay taxes to the pharaohs. Egypt also had valuable deposits of minerals, such as iron and gold, and was protected on all sides by natural boundaries - deserts, waterfalls and seas.

▲ The easiest way to travel though Egypt was by boat, on the River Nile. Boats still sail along the River Nile today (above).

A Blessed Land

Egypt's wealth, strong government and safe natural frontiers all helped a unique civilization to grow and develop. The ancient Egyptians believed that their land was very special, and had been created and blessed by the gods.

◄ The Pyramids at Giza are over 4,000 years old, but still display Egypt's wealth and power.

Proud to belong

Egyptian pharaohs grew rich, and could afford splendid palaces, temples and tombs. They also employed priests to serve in their temples, and scribes (trained writers and officials) to run their government and maintain law and order. Children born in Egypt were taught that they were lucky to belong to such a great nation.

◀ A pottery head of the child king, Tutankhamun.

EGYPTIAN LEGACY

Museums and mummies

Egypt's rich, long—lasting civilization has left a legacy of priceless treasures which still survive today, thousands of years after they were made. Visitors to Egypt can admire ancient monuments, such as temples and towering pyramid tombs. Museums in many lands house collections of ancient Egyptian statues, carvings, documents, glittering gold jewellery — and, of course, marvellous, mysterious mummies.

A New Baby

The Egyptians loved babies. Egyptian poets sang, 'Happy is the man who has a large family!' They also encouraged men to 'Marry a wife while you are young, so that she will produce a son for you ...'

Pregnancy care

During pregnancy, women from ordinary families continued to work very hard; rich women rested, and led easier lives. But all expectant mothers took extra care of themselves by rubbing their skin with oil to soften it and wearing protective amulets (lucky charms) shaped like the guardian goddesses Hequet (a frog) or Tawaret (a hippo). They also said prayers to Bes, the protector god of mothers and children. They believed that his ugly looks scared harm away from their unborn babies.

▲ The goddess Tawaret (left), shown here with a crocodile and three guardian spirits, was always portrayed with a swollen belly, like a pregnant woman.

▲ This stone carving shows two goddesses helping a queen give birth to a royal prince.

Giving birth

Mothers had their babies in a special 'birth bower' (temporary shelter made of cloth or branches, decorated with flowers), or retreated to the quietest room in the house. They gave birth squatting, supported by 'magic' bricks or a low stool, helped by other women. Soon after birth, the baby's placenta was carefully buried close to the front door of the family home, or thrown into the River Nile. Egyptians thought this would help the baby survive, by hiding traces of the birth from evil spirits.

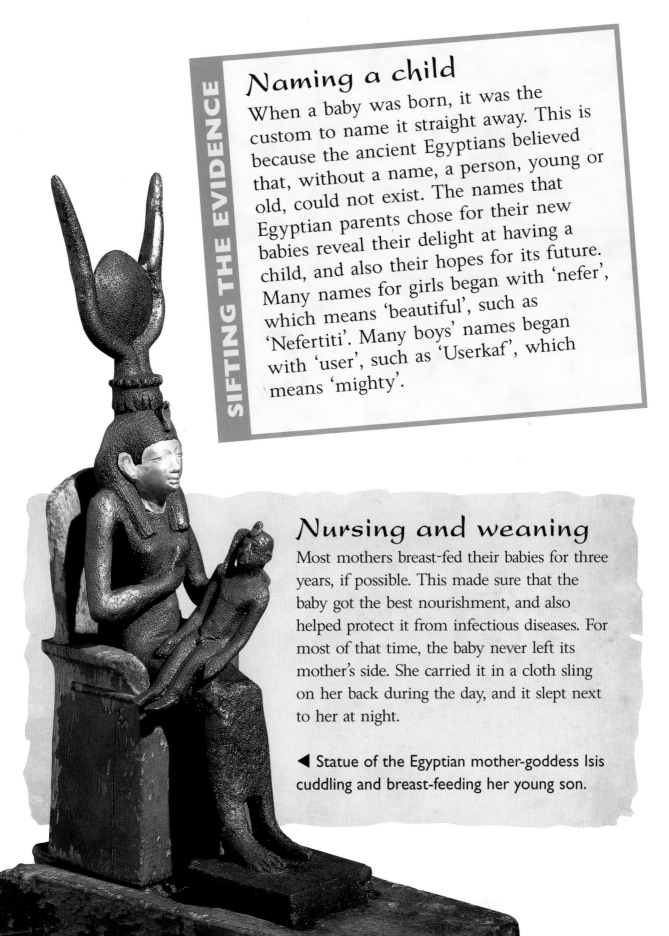

Naming a child

When a baby was born, it was the custom to name it straight away. This is because the ancient Egyptians believed that, without a name, a person, young or old, could not exist. The names that Egyptian parents chose for their new babies reveal their delight at having a child, and also their hopes for its future. Many names for girls began with 'nefer', which means 'beautiful', such as 'Nefertiti'. Many boys' names began with 'user', such as 'Userkaf', which means 'mighty'.

Nursing and weaning

Most mothers breast-fed their babies for three years, if possible. This made sure that the baby got the best nourishment, and also helped protect it from infectious diseases. For most of that time, the baby never left its mother's side. She carried it in a cloth sling on her back during the day, and it slept next to her at night.

◀ Statue of the Egyptian mother-goddess Isis cuddling and breast-feeding her young son.

7

Family Life

A new baby in Egypt would be welcomed by many relatives. Egyptian families were large and included grandparents, aunts, uncles and cousins, most of whom lived in the same village or town. Egyptians relied on their families for work, food and shelter.

Teenage parents

Egyptian families were youthful, as well as large. Many parents were teenagers. Girls got married soon after they were 12 years old, to boys just a few years older. Marriages were usually arranged by parents, although some young people wed for love. Couples hoped to have their first baby within a year of the wedding, and at least six children during their married life. If a husband and wife could not have children of their own, they adopted them.

▶ Rich men paid for loving statues of themselves and their children to be placed in tombs.

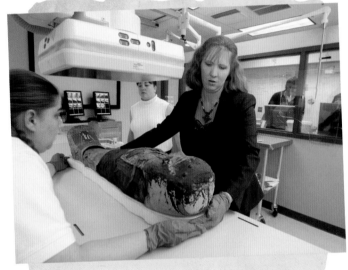

▲ Scientists scan the mummy of an Egyptian child to see how she died.

Dying young

Most Egyptians did not enjoy a long lifespan. Reaching the age of 40 was considered a good age. Many children lost their lives to infection and disease. There was a high rate of infant mortality - one death out of two or three births. To make up for this, ancient Egyptians had many children, sometimes as many as 10 to 15.

Working together

Although family life was loving, Egyptian parents expected their children to be respectful and obedient. Children also had to work alongside other family members as soon as they were able, and care for their parents if they became too old or ill to work. One Egyptian word for child, 'khered', also meant 'servant'; sons were nicknamed 'walking sticks for their fathers'.

▼ A teenage boy helps round up cattle on a farm. The pharaoh's officials would take some of them as taxes.

Investigating mummies

Archaeologists have used modern medical techniques, such as X-rays and CAT scans (see opposite), to investigate the mummies of Egyptian children. They have discovered that many young people – including teenage pharaoh Tutankhamun – died from accidental injuries. Young Egyptians suffered crushed and broken bones, or bled to death, or their wounds became badly infected. A few even had legs bitten off by hippos or crocodiles as they played in the River Nile.

Rich and Poor

Egyptian society was split into three groups. The top rank was the royal family. Next in rank came nobles, who served as ministers, army officers, priests and scribes. The lowest ranking group included farmers, labourers and craft-workers.

Like father, like son

Rank and status passed from father to son. So did ways of earning a living. There was little chance of Egyptian people changing rank from one group to another, so children grew up knowing what their future lives might be like.

Children from ordinary families - most Egyptians - expected to work hard, die young, pay taxes to the pharaoh, and, in lean times, go hungry. They hoped one day to inherit the family house. They would own only a few possessions, just some cooking pots, storage baskets, woollen blankets and farm or craft tools.

▲ A rich nobleman and his wife stand beside the tree-shaded pool in the garden surrounding their house.

▼ A tomb model of women kneading bread and baking it in an oven built from clay bricks.

In the palace

By contrast, royal children were brought up to expect the best. They lived in the beautifully-decorated royal harem (women's private palace), which was surrounded by flower-gardens and pools, and comfortably furnished with tiled floors and carved wooden beds and chairs. Some palaces even had shower-rooms and flushing lavatories.

Beyond the grave

We know that children from ordinary families sometimes went hungry because child skeletons from Egyptian burial grounds show lines of extra-thick bony tissue - called 'Harris lines' - on the bones of their feet or hands. Today, doctors know that these are signs of slower than normal growth in children, and are caused by starvation or, occasionally, serious disease.

Longer lives

Royal children spent less time with their parents than poor children, because the pharaoh and his queens were busy with official duties. Instead, they were cared for by wet-nurses and 'royal male nurses', then by servants and tutors. They might live alongside dozens of brothers and sisters; some pharaohs married over 100 wives. Just like ordinary children, royal princes and princesses were trained for their future, adult, careers. They had to carry out many royal duties, in return for their safe, comfortable living conditions, plentiful food - and (because of these) longer lives.

▶ Unlike many other pharaohs, Akhenaten (ruled 1379-1362 BC) liked to spend time with his wife and family. Here, he gently holds one of his six daughters on his knee.

Learning for Life

Once ancient Egyptian children were around four years old, they started learning skills to prepare for adult life. The skills they needed were different in towns and in the countryside, and for girls and boys.

Farming and fighting

On country farms, boys worked alongside their fathers in the fields, copying the ways that they planted, weeded and harvested crops or looked after farm animals. They also learned basic building skills. All boys were taught how to fight with sticks, spears or bows and arrows. Young men might be ordered to serve in the pharaoh's army at any time.

▶This wooden model from a tomb shows a troop of Egyptian soldiers marching off to war. All boys were expected to serve in the army.

▼ These pins, hooks, ball of yarn and weaving shuttle (yarn-holder) were used by an Egyptian woman over 2,000 years ago.

Running a home

Girls were shown by their mothers how to cook, clean, care for children, spin yarn, and weave cloth. If their families were rich, girls also had to learn how to organise and give orders to servants and slaves. Most Egyptian women spent all their time as housewives, although a few made careers managing weaving workshops or working as merchants in big towns. Some young girls trained to be musicians in temples, singers and dancers, or professional mourners.

Making and selling

In towns, boys helped in craft workshops, learning how to weave cloth, carve wood, make floor-mats, baskets and sandals from reeds, pottery from clay or jewellery from gold and precious stones. Or, if their father was a merchant who travelled from town to town, they might learn how to pack and load goods on donkeys, how to bargain and barter (swap) - the Egyptians did not use coins until around 500 BC - and how to keep accounts.

▼ Craftsmen hard at work, pictured in a wall-painting from an ancient Egyptian tomb. Children learned by watching and copying older, skilled workers like these.

Weighing gold

Painting a holy talisman (protective object)

Carrying finished goods

Carving a statue

SIFTING THE EVIDENCE

Advice to parents from Ani, an ancient Egyptian scribe

'Never grow tired of training your son ...'

'It is a son's good and blessed duty to learn and to ask ...'

'A father who spoils his son will also ruin himself ....'

'A sensible child deserves a long life ...'

13

Going to School

In ancient Egypt, education was a privilege and an honour. The chance to go to school was only given to royal children and the children of nobles and scribes. Only they would need to know how to read and write as adults. Most school pupils were boys, but some royal women were also well-educated.

Temple schools

For boys and girls, lessons in reading and writing began soon after they were four years old. They also learned simple maths. Boys were sent to live and study at schools built close to temples, where they were taught by temple priests and scribes. Royal princesses and noble girls had private lessons at home, from priestesses or trusted women tutors. Wherever they learned, pupils studied Egyptian hieroglyphs (holy writing that developed from little pictures of important people, objects and ideas).

▲ Prayers and spells written in hieroglyphs occur on many Egyptian temples and tombs.

Holy writing, magic signs

There were over 1,000 different hieroglyphs, and they were mostly used for royal, religious, magic or funeral inscriptions (carved writing). After around 2,600 BC, boys hoping to make a career as scribes also learned another script, called 'hieratic'. This was based on joined-up characters (symbols) and was much quicker and easier to write.

▲ This ancient carving shows scribes, sitting on the ground, busily writing.

Magic powers

The Egyptians believed that hieroglyphs had magic powers. So craft-workers made amulets shaped like favourite hieroglyphs, especially 'ankh', which meant 'long life'. They hoped these amulets would protect the people who wore them. 'Ankh'-shaped jewellery is still made and worn today in many parts of the world.

Reed pens stored here

Ink mixed and stored here

▲ Pupils and scribes stored pens and mixed coloured inks in palettes made from wood, baked clay or stone.

Memory training

It was very difficult to study hieroglyphs and hieratic; each separate symbol had to be recognised and memorised. Pupils learned by reading papyrus (reed-paper) scrolls and inscriptions over and over again, then reciting them from memory. They spent years practising writing, using a pen made of reeds and ink made from soot, with thin slices of wood or stone, broken bits of pottery, or expensive papyrus paper to write on. Boys who did not try their best to learn were punished. One scribe complained to a disobedient pupil, 'Although I beat you with every kind of stick, you do not listen ...'

Food and Drink

Once an Egyptian child was old enough to eat solid food, its mother or female servants prepared simple, nourishing dishes for it to eat. The amount of food, and the range of foodstuffs available, depended on each family's wealth and social status.

Gritty bread

Children did not eat much of the Egyptians' most important food, bread, until they had a full set of teeth. Bread was made from wheat grains crushed on stone slabs, mixed with water, kneaded by hand, shaped into loaves, then baked in mud-brick ovens. It was often full of grit from the griding-stones, and sand from the desert. It could be very tough and chewy; mummies show that it quickly wore away people's teeth.

◀ A tomb model shows women grinding grain into to flour, ready to make bread.

Favourite foods

Favourite foods for newly-weaned babies included vegetables, such as the fleshy stems of papyrus reeds. When children were a little bit older, they might be given gruel (thin porridge) made from wheat or barley stewed with water and sweetened with honey or dates. Young boys and girls ate with their mothers and other women, after the men had finished eating.

▶ Geese and ducks – shown here – were favourite foods, but only rich families could afford them.

▲ Egyptians straining beer through a pottery sieve.

Soupy beer

Young children were allowed to sip the ancient Egyptians' most important drink: thick, sweet, soupy beer. This contained very little alcohol. It was made from water, mixed with slices of bread then left to ferment (bubble) in the sun. Sometimes, fruit was added as flavouring. If properly prepared, beer was nourishing and filling, and might replace solid food at some mealtimes.

Rationing

Workers building pharaohs' tombs in the Valley of the Kings around 1500-1000 BC were issued with food rations by the government, for themselves and their families. Records of these survive, and tell us what Egyptian family meals were like. Wheat or barley were the most important items in the diet, together wih beans, onions, garlic, fresh salad vegetables such as lettuces and cucumbers, and salted fish. Meat was a luxury, eaten only on special occasions.

Clothes and Hairstyles

For the first few years of their lives, boys and girls in Ancient Egypt wore no clothes at all. This was clean and hygenic for babies, but also comfortable for toddlers and older children in Egypt's hot, dry climate.

Free to play

Children did not begin to wear clothes until they were almost grown up, around 10 to 12 years old. Adult clothes would have made it awkward for young children to run around and move freely. They would also have been difficult for mothers or servants to keep clean, after children had been playing in muddy fields or dusty yards, or splashing about beside the River Nile.

▶ A naked girl servant helps a rich woman to put on her clothes and jewellery.

Jewellery, make-up, hairstyles

Although children wore no clothes, they shared the Egyptian love of jewellery, make-up and hair styling. Ancient statues show young children wearing all kinds of protective amulets, together with decorative girdles (belts), and necklaces, bracelets and ankle-bands of pearls, shells, coral, glass or rough pottery beads. Boys and girls wore their hair in a special children's style, known as the 'sidelock of youth'. Most of their hair was cropped short, but several strands were left hanging, braided together, above the right ear.

◀ This stylish young woman, shown on a wall painting wears a long curly wig, a wide jewelled necklace and thick eyeliner.

Adult styles

Once children were old enough to marry, they began to wear clothes in adult styles. Egyptian garments were mostly long rectangles of wool or linen cloth wrapped loosely around the body. Men wore knee-length kilts, with or without fancy pleats at the front, and a cloak thrown over the shoulders. At first, women wore long, straight shifts, later, after about 1500 BC, they preferred loose robes of finely-pleated linen.

▲ A wall painting showing Egyptian men wearing cloth kilts. One of them has their hairstyled in a distinctive side lock.

EGYPTIAN LEGACY

Make-up

The Egyptian fashion for heavy lines of dark green or grey kohl (a sticky paste of crushed metal and oil) above and below the eye, has been copied several times in past centuries. It became very popular in the 1960s after Holywood star Elizabeth Taylor wore Egyptian-style eyeliner for the film *Cleopatra*. More recently, singer Amy Winehouse has also chosen to make-up her eyes like an ancient Egyptian beauty.

Sports and Games

All children, rich and poor, spent their free time playing - mostly, out of doors in Egypt's warm, dry climate. Play was fun, but it also helped train boys and girls for their adult duties.

Sport for all

Stone carvings and wall-paintings show children and teenagers running races, playing leap-frog and tug-of-war, juggling with balls, dancing, leaping and performing acrobatics. Boys also went swimming and fishing in the River Nile, rode donkeys, practised shooting with bows and arrows, and took part in other war-games, such as boxing, wrestling and fighting with sticks.

▲ Fishing – with a multi-pronged spear (left) and a net (right) on the banks of the Nile.

Dolls and model animals

Favourite toys included dolls, puppets, spinning tops, rattles, balls, blowpipes and model animals on wheels or with mouths that snapped open and shut. Some toys were rough and home made; others were expensive, and neatly crafted by skilled workers. The poorest children played with anything they could find, such as pebbles, feathers, or scraps of wood or cloth. Children also made model monsters, houses, boats and mummies out of sticky mud; some of these have been found by archaeologists excavating the remains of workers' houses.

▼ This pull-along ancient Egyptian horse, made from wood, looks very like similar toys today.

SIFTING THE EVIDENCE

Not just toys

Board games, such as senet (rather like draughts), and painted wooden dolls have been found in ancient Egyptian tombs. Archaeologists think that these were not children's toys, but games with magic meanings. Senet symbolised the passage of a dead person's soul through the Afterlife, and all the dangers that might kill it. The dolls were either symbols of loving female companionship, or fertility symbols to bring 'life force' into the tomb and help the dead live again.

▼ This senet board has a useful drawer to store the pieces after the game is over.

Animals

Egyptian families kept pets for pleasure and companionship, and farm animals because they were useful. They also admired the strength and beauty of wild creatures, and worshipped many gods in animal form.

Household companions

Most Egyptian children grew up alongside well-loved family pets. Cats, dogs, birds and monkeys were favourites. Like children, pets were expected to help their family. Cats protected farmers' grain-stores from rats and mice. Dogs kept watch over flocks of sheep, houses and workshops, or helped huntsmen track and catch deer in the desert. Caged birds sang sweetly; monkeys might be trained to help farmers and gardeners by picking ripe fruit from the topmost branches of trees.

▼ This baboon has been painted with his hands raised in prayer, as if he were human.

Pet sounds

What did Egyptian cats and dogs sound like? We know from their names. In the ancient Egyptian language, cats were called 'miw', and dogs were called 'iw iw' (which sounds rather like a high-pitched bark). The words 'cat' and 'dog' also featured in nicknames. One famous pharaoh was called Pamiu, which means tomcat(!), and royal prisoners were often known as 'the pharaoh's dogs'.

At work on the farm

Country children played with, gathered food for and helped to look after, many farm animals. Egyptians kept sheep to provide wool and goats for milking. Cattle gave meat, milk, and skins to make leather; oxen (heavy cattle) provided power to pull carts and ploughs. Young lambs, goat-kids and calves all might be killed for luxury meals on special occasions; meat from oxen was highly prized for sacrifices to the gods. Some farmers raised pigs, but many Egyptians thought that pigs and their keepers were unclean.

▲ A boy milks a cow, while she licks her young calf (right) tenderly.

Transport and taxes

▼ This is a wall-painting from an Egyptian tomb. Oxen did most of the heavy work around farms, and were also used as transport.

Children fed ducks and geese and gathered their eggs, as well as caring for the donkeys used to pull carts, carry heavy loads or ride on. Only very rich families could afford to own horses, which did not survive well in Egypt's hot, dry environment. Camels, which originated in Asia, were not known on farms in Egypt until around 800 BC. As well as providing food, power and transport, animals were also often used to pay farm taxes.

Religion

Egyptian people, young and old, believed that the gods protected their land. In return, they honoured gods and goddesses with prayers, sacrifices and holy festivals, to ask for continued help and protection.

Praying together

From as early as they could remember, Egyptian children took part in family worship. Most homes had a little statue or picture of a guardian god, where families said prayers or left little offerings (gifts) of food. The most popular household god was Bes, guardian of mothers and babies, but families might sometimes honour a favourite local god or spirit, such as Bastet (the cat-goddess) in northern Egypt, or Sobek (the crocodile god) in the south.

▲ Giant statues of Pharaoh Rameses II (ruled 1292-1225 BC) guard the entrance to this massive temple at Abu Simbel, southern Egypt.

Forbidden temples

Temples were the homes of the gods; only pharaohs, priests and priestesses could enter their sacred courtyards and secret inner shrines. However, children would have been among the crowds that gathered to watch huge, beautiful statues of gods and goddesses being carried out from temples in holy processions on festival days.

▲ A carving of the ancient Egyptian god Bes at Philae Temple, an island in the River Nile near Aswan.

Jealous ghosts, evil demons

Although they honoured and trusted the gods, Egyptian people also feared many unseen forces that threatened their families. They said magic spells, wore magic belts or beads and trusted the magic number seven to protect them. They made loud noises by stamping, shouting, shaking rattles or banging drums to help drive dangerous ghosts or demons away.

◄ A scarab amulet, worn to ward off evil spirits.

SIFTING THE EVIDENCE

Magic spells

When children fell ill, parents prayed or chanted magic spells like this:

'Come out, crawling demon from the darkness, you with the head that faces backwards, not forwards...

Are you here to do this child harm? You must not!

Have you come to take it away? You must not!'

Everlasting Life

Death was never far away in ancient Egypt, even for children. Egyptian parents believed their children might have a chance to be reborn in the Otherworld, so long as its body was carefully preserved.

▲ This mummy case was made to preserve the body of a rich young girl, and help her to live for ever.

Wealthy people

Wealthy people could afford to have the bodies of their dead children made into mummies. Mothers and babies who died during childbirth were mummified together; otherwise, children's mummies were separate. Dead children's bodies were cleaned, dried, coated with protective oils and resins, wrapped in bandages then laid to rest in a decorated coffin. Toys, amulets, jewellery and other treasures were gently placed beside them, and a tall stele (carved stone pillar) might record their name.

Ordinary people

Ordinary families wrapped their dead children in linen cloth or mats of woven palm-tree leaves, before burying them in cemeteries. These were sited on the outskirts of towns, or on the west bank of the River Nile. Some familes chose instead to bury their dead children under the floor of their houses.

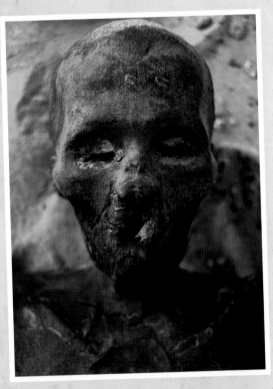

▲ The preserved mummy of an Egyptian child.

Offerings

All families buried their dead children with prayers and offerings, and some continued to make offerings at a child's tomb for many years, to 'feed' its spirit. This was a powerful way of keeping the family together, by linking the living and the dead.

▼ This ancient Egyptian wall painting shows mourners at the head of a funeral procession.

SIFTING THE EVIDENCE

Remembering the dead

Inscriptions from Egyptian children's tombs:

'The dark, that frightens children, swallowed me up...'

'I was loved by my father, cherished by my mother. My brothers and sisters all loved me...'

Activities

Why not experience some of the things that Egyptian children did, by trying some of these activities?

Jewelled Collars

Rich Egyptians wore magnificent collar-shaped necklaces, made of gold and jewels. You can see part of one on page 18. Try making an Egyptian-style necklace:

You will need:

- Gold or yellow card, about 30 cm x 30 cm
- Pen or pencil
- Compasses
- Scissors
- Glue
- Sequins, plastic 'jewels', or glittery stickers, or stick-on leaves and flower shapes
- Hole punch
- Ribbon or cord about 50 cm long

1. Use the pen or pencil and compasses to draw a half-circle on the card of about 15 cm radius. Cut around the long curved edge.

2. Mark the mid-point of the long edge of the card. From this, draw a second half circle, of about 8 cm radius. Cut it out.

3. Fix sequins, plastic jewels, glitter stickers or flower and leaf shapes on the curved card shape you have made.

4. Punch a hole at each end of the inner half circle. Thread ribbon or cord through and tie it at the back of your neck.

Scarab Amulet

Many Egyptians carried these charms with them, for good luck. Why not make a holy scarab beetle? You will need:

- Self-hardening clay
- Modelling tool
- Paint
- Brushes
- Glue
- Beads

1. Find a picture of a scarab amulet in a book (see below) or website about ancient Egypt.

2. Make a beetle-body shape (an oval dome) out of clay.

3. At one end, make two hollows, for eyes. Mark the wings on the scarab's back and the legs, along its sides.

4. When the clay is dry, paint the scarab and stick on beads for eyes.

Egyptian Picnic Food

Egyptian people enjoyed boating trips and picnics beside the River Nile. Try these favourite Egyptian picnic foods:

1. Wholemeal pitta bread, warmed then filled with chopped lettuce, cucumber and mashed sardines. [Egyptians would have used river-fish, instead.] Tasty!

2. Brown bread sandwich filled with low-fat cream cheese, chopped dates and honey. Yum!

3. Fresh, sweet, juicy melon slices or chunks. Delicious!

Your Name in Hieroglyphs

There are several websites that will automatically translate your name and your friends' names into hieroglyphs. Look at the list on page 30. You could also choose a famous Egyptian name such as Rameses (for a boy) or Cleopatra (for a girl) and see how these would have looked when written down. To find more ancient Egyptian names to translate, look in the index of any book about ancient Egypt.

Egyptian Happy Families

Make some playing cards with pictures of Egyptian people on them, and play Happy Families, Egyptian-style.

You will need:

- 24 plain white postcards
- Pens, pencils, felt-tips or paints

1. Divide the cards into six sets, each containing four cards.

2. Think of six different kinds of Egyptian families. The following list might help you:

- Gods
- Scribes
- Farmers
- Royal family
- Craft-workers
- Servants

3. Draw pictures on each set of four cards of four family members (Mother, Father, Boy, Girl) from each family type. Write names for each family member.

4. Deal out the cards between players. The player whose turn it is asks another player for a specific card; the asker must already hold at least one card of the same family. If the player asked has the card it must be handed over and the asker continues by asking the same or another player for another card. If the player does not have the card they say 'not at home' and the turn passes to them. Completed families are placed face down in front of the owner. When all families are complete, the player with most families, wins.

Timeline

6000-3100 BC **Pre-dynastic Period** Farmers settle in Egypt. They build villages beside River Nile.

3100-2686 BC **Early Dynastic Period** King Narmer unites northern and southern Egypt into one kingdom. First capital city at Menphis. Hieroglyphs invented.

2682-2181 BC **Old Kingdom** Age of strong pharaohs and growing wealth. Great pyramids built.

2181-2055 BC **First Intermediate Period** A troubled time. Pharaohs are weak and Eygpt is divided.

2055-1650 BC **Middle Kingdom** Egypt conquers Nubia (now Sudan). Pharaohs pay for magnificent temples and statues. Capital city moves to Thebes.

1650-1550 BC **Second Intermediate Period** Hyksos (settlers from West Asia) take control of Egypt. Pharaohs win back control in 1567 BC.

1550-1069 BC **New Kingdom** Pharaohs, such as Rameses II, conquer a great empire. Trade grows with South and East Africa and in lands around the Mediterranean Sea. Many great works of art, including Tutankhamun's tomb in the Valley of the Kings. Coastal lands in the Eastern Mediterranean are invaded. Pharaoh Rameses defeats them in 1198 BC.

1069-747 BC **Third Intermediate Period** Egypt divided. Assyrians invade from the Middle East. Kings from Nubia invade and rule southern Egypt.

747-332 BC **Late Period** Pharaohs grow weak. Invaders from Persia (now Iran) conquer Egypt in 525 BC.

332-30 BC **Ptolemaic Period** Alexander the Great, King of Macedon (north of Greece) invades and conquers Egypt. Greek-speaking Macedonian kings and queens (including Cleopatra) rule.

30 BC-395 AD **Roman Period** Egypt is conquered by Rome, and becomes part of the Roman Empire.

Glossary and further information

amulet Lucky charm.

barter Swap or exchange.

bower Small, enclosed, private space.

ferment Bubble, fizz, and eventually turn into alcohol. Fermentation is caused by yeasts (micro-organisms).

harem Separate living quarters for women.

hieratic Script that used joined-up symbols and was quick to write.

hieroglyphs Holy script that used little picture-symbols of people, objects and ideas.

girdle Belt, often worn low on the hips.

kohl Sticky paste made of oil and crushed metal, used as eyeliner.

mourner People who suffer grief when a dead loved one dies, or who are paid to weep and wail at funerals.

palette Flat, smooth piece of wood or stone, used to mix paint or ink on.

parasites Creatures who take nourishment from a 'host' species, for example, by sucking their blood.

placenta Body-part that develops inside a mother's womb during pregnancy. It helps food and oxygen pass from the mother to the unborn baby.

reeds Tall grass-like plants that grow in damp places. Papyrus is made from reeds.

resin Gum from plants.

sacrifices Offerings to the gods, to give thanks or ask for favours.

scribes Trained writers who often worked as government officials.

shrine Holy place.

stele Carved stone pillar.

weaning Teaching a young baby to change from drinking milk all the time to eating solid foods.

wet-nurses Women paid to breast-feed another woman's baby.

Further information

www.ancientegypt.co.uk/menu.html The British Museum website. Unwrap a mummy, see the wonderful exhibits, and learn what it was like to live in Egypt thousands of years ago.

www.bbc.co.uk/history/ancient/egyptians/ A site from the BBC, full of fascinating information.

www.pbs.org/empires/egypt/index.html A site from the USA Public Broadcasting Service; includes an interactive map, a hieroglyph translator and a timeline.

www.eyelid.co.uk/ Includes reconstructions of temples, Egyptian maths, Egyptian games and how to write your name in hieroglyphs.

www.besthistorysites.net/AncientBiblical_Egypt.shtml A site listing many more great websites about ancient Egypt.

Index